To Eleanor
Who foster's earth's future
one human at a time—

thanks as always for Being

Karl

Dedicated to my parents,
Dorothy and Richard Roberts,
for bringing me into this wonder of life,
and to Peggy Ferris,
my friend and book designer.

Passions and Patience

Fostering Earth's Future Through Unlikely Partnerships

BY
KAREN ROBERTS

PRINCIPAL PHOTOGRAPHER
TIM HAUF

Passions and Patience
Fostering Earth's Future through Unlikely Partnerships
Published by Gaia & friends, Inc
464 Meadowbrook Drive Santa Barbara, CA 93018
Principal Photographer Tim Hauf
Text by Karen Roberts
Edited by Cheryl Carnahan & Susan Gardner
Book Design by Peggy Ferris Design
email: peggyferris@cox.net
www.karenrobertsauthor.com

ISBN 0-9746449-1-1 (softbound) ISBN 0-9746449-2-7 (hardbound)
Library of Congress Control Number 2004100181
First Printing 2004
Printed and bound in Korea.

Preceding Spread: Woman in Nepal.
Above: California oak woodland in Gaviota.

Table of *Contents*

Above: *Surfer waiting for wave in Gaviota.*

Fostering Earth's Future Through Unlikely Partnerships

This planet's current ecological crisis is without precedent. Nature has experienced massive devastation at the hands of humankind, and we cannot avoid confrontation with the evidence. Our daily newspapers and nightly news programs bombard us with illustrations of the disastrous results of our actions. We feel guilty about our transgressions and hopeless about our power to reverse the damage. Many people are too fearful to even look at the wreckage, much less take steps to change what has happened. They believe that, as individuals, there isn't anything they can do. However, nothing could be further from the truth.

Individuals can, and do, make a difference. One individual can speak out, others listen and add their voices, and an alliance is born. This grassroots activity of local people with local leadership is powerful. It begins with individuals talking with their neighbors, reaching over the fences to make connection. When people gather they listen to each other's experiences and learn from one another. This local-level dialogue is the first step toward exercising influence for the purpose of change.

The fine art of collaboration is the next step. Even groups working for the same cause may have different points of view, different ideas of the direction to take at any given point. Unfortunately, our schools don't generally teach us the skills needed for negotiating agreement without forfeiting position. But negotiate we must if our mission is to be successful. What is the blueprint for change? We must let go of preconceived ideas and stay committed to the process of finding common ground. It is not through winning but through collaborating that true change can take root.

Coming to agreement with strangers with contrary opinions requires acceptance and respect. The work may seem interminable—hours spent

sitting in a room, returning to the table again and again with hopes of progress. The dialogue may be contentious. In these instances, patience becomes a commodity as important as understanding. Research demonstrates that three qualities are present in successful collaborative projects: passion, patience, and the willingness to work it out. The combination of these three elements can lead to a new direction, one that is acceptable to all and can be presented as the grassroots position for agencies or governments to follow.

In recent decades, many marvelous stories have emerged of those who were willing to negotiate, to talk before acting. There were individuals and groups that previously considered themselves archenemies but continued working together until they found a common ground. They didn't carry boastful banners on Earth Day or announce that they were saving the world, yet the state of the world has indeed been bettered through their efforts. In neighboring communities and across borders, they negotiated their differences in order to reach their goals. *Passions and Patience* celebrates their work.

Philosophers, scientists, and poets have written of the web of life, the interrelatedness of all living beings, and also of the possessive and territorial nature of the individual. It is clear that our planet cannot survive if we selfishly continue to participate as global investors and consumers, not realizing our complicity in the diseased state of the Earth. This book is about those people who took a huge step and crossed over into the territory of interrelatedness, of sharing, of giving up what they previously considered essential to self. Through this collection of photos and essays I celebrate their spirit and present you with their stories—and, in turn, with hope.

Above: *Gaviota coastline, California.*

Above: *North Dakota farm, an example of land set aside for preservation of habitat for wildlife.*

CHAPTER ONE

For the Birds

NORTHERN GREAT PLAINS IN AMERICA AND CANADA

> *"Like winds and sunsets, wild things were taken for granted*
> *Until progress began to do away with them.*
> *Now we face the question whether a still higher 'standard of living'*
> *Is worth its cost in things natural, wild and free.*
> *For us in the minority, the opportunity to see geese*
> *Is more important than television,*
> *And the chance to find a pasque-flower*
> *Is a right as inalienable as free speech."*
>
> –Aldo Leopold, Foreword to A Sand County Almanac

Lots of folks care about birds. Children fashion duck houses, a small town in Minnesota observes Prairie Potholes Day, and sportsmen throughout the land take their guns to the blinds. Each occasion is a celebration of the waterfowl and the distinctive wetland habitat that is a major part of the environment in the Great Plains, as evidenced by the multitude of names scientists and locals have assigned them: pond, slough, shallow lake, and prairie pothole.

Aldo Leopold (1887-1948) was a scholar who was well aware of broad-based interest in the environment. He earned his Master's Degree in Forestry from Yale in 1909 and chaired the first university-level wildlife management department from its inception at the University of Wisconsin in 1933 until his death 15 years later. Internationally rec-

Above: A slough no longer under cultivation due to program of the United States Farm Bill to restore wetlands.

ognized as the father of modern wildlife management and ecology, he authored *A Sand County Almanac*, a book widely accepted as the "environmentalist's bible." That and Leopold's classic text, *Game Management*, are still used today.

Leopold knew that concerns for wildlife issues existed well beyond the confines of the college classroom, and he wrote of the unique beauties and complexities of tall grass ecosystems. His studies of watersheds, wildlife, and soils have instructed not only policy makers but also the public. His students recognized that an effective conservationist works cooperatively with private landowners, building community support.

During the latter part of his career, Leopold devoted his energies to various conservation and leisure clubs, remembering the hunting ethics his grandfather had taught him. For Leopold, sportsmanship was an honorable pursuit when it followed certain rules and responsibilities. For example, bow hunting became his preference as a purer form of sport, giving the game a fairer chance. When hired by a sporting ammunitions company, Leopold conducted the first official survey of game populations and of the effectiveness of each state's conservation efforts. His studies showed a clear connection between species populations and the availability of food and cover.

Preservation of America's wildlife came to be Leopold's primary focus. Early in the budding field of ecology and conservation, Leopold presented a novel idea to Americans—the game cooperative. He convinced hunters and farmers to improve their lands for the sake of the birds. When given the opportunity to bring more income onto the farm by stocking some wild game, using land management techniques, and selling hunting fees, farmers became willing participants in the preservation of wildlife populations. Leopold later commented on the success of the venture, recounting how, strolling over formerly game-less farms, the quail now whistled in every fence row and pheasant cocks crowed. Scientists, conservationists, sportsmen, and farmers experimented with working together in game cooperatives and discovered the resultant benefits for humans and wildlife alike.

Above: *Waterfowl at home in classic wetland in North Dakota.*

Above: *Canadian geese feeding and farmer tilling with his tractor—the long-sought understanding of those various elements in the North American Waterfowl Management Plan.*
Opposite, above and below: *Prairie grasses, Grasslands National Park, Saskatchewan, Canada.*

Perennial native grasses, the heart and soul of the prairie, had been sacrificed to agriculture, but new awareness and new methods of countering the trend are making a difference. In the several generations since Leopold's first writings, ecology has become familiar to the public as a basic understanding of a system of natural balance, of the interrelatedness of all parts. Unlikely partnerships of gun makers and scientists, farmers and decoy designers, dog trainers and bird watchers found common cause in keeping the waterfowl coming.

One of Leopold's students, Art Hawkins, is now a patriarch of wildlife management and conservation. A large man with twinkling eyes and a slight smile, Hawkins is a scientist who "lives the land ethic" in the tradition of Leopold's teachings. These days, he and his wife of sixty-plus years live on the side of a lake in Minnesota where over the years, they have applied their knowledge and abundant creative energies to recovering an overgrown slough. To protect the pond as a duck habitat, they've gone to court to confront real estate developers; to provide the nesting grass for the waterfowl, they've planted a prairie.

Prairie grasses depend on regular fires, called "controlled burns," to keep invading trees and bushes away. We had planned a visit to the Hawkins' home, and the timing of our arrival fortuitously occurred after a "good burn." The grass stood four feet tall in a bouquet of varying types. Dried flowers and seeded stems covered the grasses and the nests of waterfowl from seasons past. Guiding us over the land that afternoon, Hawkins brought to life for us the possibility of prairie restoration and the reality of a duckland preserved. The ethic of wildlife management and conservation that originated with Leopold has been carried forth by Hawkins in his work with the United States Fish and Wildlife Department and in his own backyard.

Left, above: *Prairie pothole in North Dakota with caattails and ducks.*
below: *Mendosa Mallard at home in reeds in Alberta, Canada.*

Above: *Grain planted for wildlife in North Dakota, part of the Grasslands for Tomorrow Program of the United States Farm Bill, designed to provide habitat for grassland nesting birds.*

The future of the waterfowl and prairies depends upon future generations. A tradition of responsible waterfowling is not inbred, so programs for the young must be the beginning. Numerous nature centers have responded to this need by establishing experiential nature programs. Children can explore wetlands and waterfowl by participating in conservation projects and games and even by walking through the shallow waters. Young waterfowlers throughout the state of Minnesota gather at Woody Camp, a prairie wetlands learning center. The camp provides a cooperative learning environment, fostering teamwork while teaching environmental science and practical hunting skills. Ducks Unlimited offers the Greenwing Program, and Pheasants Forever offers the Leopold Education Program. Learning the habits of ducks, or the art of working with decoys, or the way to load black-powder muzzle guns are all of equal fascination to a child. Even those born and raised in the city or suburbs can establish an intimacy with their natural legacy and perhaps carry on the heritage of involvement with wildlife by becoming tomorrow's conservation leaders.

Above: *Art Hawkins, student of Aldo Leopold, still passing on the teachings of* A Sand County Almanac, *of wildlife management and conservation.*
Below right: *Daughter of Art Hawkins collected these hen houses on the family property in Minnesota.*
Opposite: *Blue-winged teal, one of the many duck species that make their nests in the grasses of the Great Plains of North America.*

Aldo Leopold's words echo again:

I heard of a boy who was brought an atheist.
He changed his mind when he saw
There were a hundred-odd species of warblers,
Each bedecked like the rainbow,
And each performing thousands of miles of migration
About which scientists wrote wisely but did not understand.

(from *Goose Music,* A Sand County Almanac)

Above: *Hverarond geothermal field.*

CHAPTER TWO

Kick the Oil Habit

ICELAND

> "No higher than the soul is high
> The world stands out on either side
> No wider than Passions and Patience;
> Above the world is stretched the sky."
>
> —Edna St.Vincent Millay, *from* Renassence

Iceland, known as the "Land of Fire and Ice," is marked by an ever-changing landscape of volcanoes, steaming fissures, and thermal water pools amid snow and glaciers.

We went there not only to discover the stunning beauty and mystery of the country but to meet with the managing director of New Energy Ltd., Jon Bjorn Skulason, in Reykjavik, the nation's capital, which with its population of a mere 160,000 is one of the smallest capitals in the world. New Energy, a consortium of DaimlerChrysler, Shell, and Norsk Hydro, isn't large either, but its business is steadily growing larger. This alliance of business, government, and academic institutions exists because of the vision of an Icelandic chemistry professor, Professor Bragi Arnason, who as a student thirty years ago mapped Iceland's reservoirs of hot groundwater under a glacier as part of his doctoral thesis in chemistry.

The huge reservoirs of natural geothermal energy he found eventually will generate the power to make hydrogen fuel. This new fuel, a bottomless well of clean energy, will emit only water mist. Arnason's studies became so important that they are presently responsible for making his country the world leader in hydrogen power. That the beginning of the next major shift in the world's energy source would come from a far corner of the world is not surprising if one looks at the history of that remote, ice-bound country.

Iceland long ago was forced to explore alternative energy sources because of the prohibitive cost of importing fossil fuels to this remote island country. The cold winds of long, dark winters increase fuel demand for heating homes and running the country's large fleets of fishing boats. Norwegian Vikings had settled here over a millennium ago, and settlement by the sea has remained the natural way of life. The people of Iceland have always been independent and hardy, and dependence on imported oil for gas-guzzling fishing vessels, although unavoidable, tied Iceland's economy to the world's volatile supplies and prices. From 1944 to 1995 the small island country struggled with mounting inflation, creating pressure for some final energy solution.

Right: *Hverarond geothermal field.*

Above: *Grindavik, the Blue Lagoon. In the background, Svgartsengi geothermal power plant produces such clean energy that humans swim next to the power plants.*

The world's subterranean pressures crack the surface of Iceland, causing mountains to rise, horizons to change. Enormous reserves of natural geothermal energy are contained in this dynamic landscape. In the early 1970s, Arnason went to the top of one of the glaciers to map the reservoirs of hot groundwater as part of his chemistry thesis. In 1978, he delivered his first paper on hydrogen, exploring his idea of using it as a fuel source. People laughed at his idea, calling him a mad scientist, even though the United States Space Program at the time was using hydrogen fuel. Arnason's proposal for use of hydrogen cells for everyday use seemed unrealistic to most experts. However, one visiting professor assured him his work was promising, and Arnason began speaking to Rotary clubs, his classes, and many other small groups, not only discussing his belief in an environmentally friendly hydrogen-fueled future but backing it up with enough hard data to enough listeners that he became a catalyst into the twenty-first century for a true change in energy use. A researcher at the auto company that is now Daimler-Benz was one of those intrigued listeners.

Oil company Royal Dutch Shell took interest as well, recognizing the need to be prepared for the future as well as the need to clean up its soiled image as a polluting industry.

Thus, the unlikely alliance of an oil company, a gas-powered combustion-engine auto company, and an isolated nation to develop hydrogen fuel cells was born. It became Icelandic New Energy Ltd., each of the players embarking on a novel scientific enterprise, marking a definite departure from their prior businesses. This joint venture plans to deliver three hydrogen buses and a new fueling station by 2004.

Iceland is an ideal testing ground for this new energy, with two-thirds of the country's energy consumption already coming from geothermal and hydroelectric power plants. These are both renewable and inexpensive while being clean. Such advantages in the small island country give it a unique advantage in the production of hydrogen as a new energy.

Top: *Grindavik, Svgartsengi geothermal power plant.*
Bottom: *Myvatn, Krafla geothermal power station.*
Sheep graze safely nearby.

Above: *Icelandic ponies on the Snaefellsnes Peninsula.*

Iceland's small size also enhances its status as a model. The three buses purchased for public transit represent five percent of the nation's fleet, and the country's entire transportation system can be modified for a relatively small investment. In 25 to 30 years, Iceland plans to use hydrogen cells to power all of its cars, buses, and fishing fleet. The Icelandic people have supported change in energy sources before, embracing the introduction of both hydroelectric and geothermal power in the last half century. Although the complete transformation to hydrogen cells will not be realized in the lifetime of Arnason, he states unequivocally, "My children will see the transformation, and my grandchildren will live in the new economy."

According to New Energy's Skulason, the Ecological City Transport System (ECTOS) plans delivery of the buses from DaimlerChrysler in 2003 and to erect a hydrogen fueling station in Reykjavik by Shell Iceland to accompany the use of the buses. Commercial stations will come later, probably alongside the introduction of cars that have not been developed yet. The problem of chickens and eggs, one coming before the other, will be the real-time experience of introducing a new fuel to the public in whatever country. The infrastructure needs to be set up at the same time the technology is put on the road. New Energy's combined research and demonstration project, establishing an infrastructure as well as a fleet, is being undertaken simultaneously and on a relatively small budget.

Other countries of the European Union have taken active interest in New Energy's operations, not only by ordering buses but also through working within their government's energy-planning departments. In the United States, California's Fuel Cell Partnership was joined in June 2002 by the United States Environmental Protection Agency in a public/private venture to demonstrate and promote fuel-cell vehicles as a commercially viable, environmentally sound venture. The partners of California Fuel Cell Partnership include automobile makers DaimlerChrysler, Ford, GM, Honda, Hyundai, Toyota, and Volkswagen and the energy companies BP, Shell, and Texaco. Governor Schwarznegger's transportation policy for California included the creation of a costly string of 200 hydrogen filling stations along freeways and highways throughout the state. His vision is similar to Professor Arnason's; conversion to hydrogen from fossil fuels is not a question of whether, but when.

Above: *Eastern Iceland, Lagarfoss hydro-power station.*

Involvement of U.S. government agencies such as the Department of Energy and the Department of Transportation is making the coming decade's story of hydrogen fuel cells a more likely success. Twenty years ago, when first the idea of hydrogen fuel cells was discussed, the lack of support at both public and private levels killed the concept. Now the publicity at many levels, including actor Dennis Weaver's letter to President Bush urging him to plan for a conversion to hydrogen for the health of the children, is forcing people in power to think about the alternatives.

The need for more definite support with funding from the federal government in the United States is a response to the people who have demanded cleaner air and greater security. Whether oil involves the world in another war or not, such is the constant fear worldwide. Arnason and Ballard CEO Rasul have been catalysts for change. Cleaner and more efficient automobiles have been envisioned by these men, who rallied private enterprise and public opinion; political will, as in Iceland, is the tougher agent. In Iceland it has been the strong will of the people that has forced government support of the vision of a hydrogen-based future. Skulason is an excellent manager for the consortium, proving once again that individuals make the alliances that negotiate success.

Above: *Western fjords, Atlantic Puffin.*
Right: *Western fjords, Dynjandi waterfalls.*

Above: *South Coast, Porsmork.*

Above: *Northeast Iceland, Myvatlin.*

Above: *Terraces of croplands, village of Kharikhala.*

CHAPTER THREE

Glorious Peaks

HIMALAYAN NEPAL

> "A sense of responsibility toward all others also means that, both as individuals and as a society of individuals, we have a duty to care for each member of our society."
> –His Holiness the Dalai Lama, from
> Ethics for the New Millennium

Nepal has survived as a deeply spiritual civilization in a very harsh climate and landscape for thousands of years. The first Westerners did not arrive until 1951. Two years later Sir Edmund Hillary and Tenzing Norgay, his Sherpa companion, toiled to the top of Mt. Everest (29,035 feet) in the first successful climb of the daunting peak, securing a place in history and bringing the attention of the world to Nepal.

In the last 50 years the cloistered, secretive country has been marked not only by opening borders to Western influence but by the pressures of population and poverty. Previously the people of Nepal lived in balance with nature, despite the despotic rule of the Rana family for 104 years. Temples and prayer flags were the cultural and socioeconomic statements of the Hindu and Buddhist peoples. Farming, though always undertaken at a subsistence level, provided a decent living and was complemented by customs of celebration and daily spirituality. Travelers to Nepal always return with stories of the cheer of the native people and their unquestioning generosity.

Above: *Monkey Temple in Kathmandu,*
honored by prayer flags.

Above: *World Wildlife Fund sign in background, Buddhist Mani Rock in
foreground—both acknowledging reforestation project. The partnership of the
World Wildlife Fund, the Himalayan Trust, and local community forest groups
has planted over 100,000 tree seedlings a year.*

Tourism has since developed as the nation's primary industry. Trekkers come from all over the world, serious to make an ascent of Everest. Others come to enjoy what once was considered to be Shangri-La, a land of beauty and ease. As a result, Kathmandu, the city in which to begin either of these tourist pursuits, now has one of the most polluted climates in the world. The trinket shops that proliferate even in the small villages provide little reward for "shopkeepers," and the Sherpa guides don't get paid enough to sustain their families at even minimal levels.

In the other parts of the country, agriculture predominates. Because farming is undertaken at a family level, it has remained unchanged for generations, yet recent population pressures and increasing soil infertility have led to paltry crops and dehumanizing poverty. The average income, as stated in a *National Geographic* article of November 2000, is $210 a year. Farmers who needed additional land took over jungle acreage after the government used DDT to kill off mosquitoes, but this new land did not remain fertile. Nepal's launch into the modern world from a medieval state a generation ago was not met by the learned wisdom of farming techniques with modern technology. Unfortunately, the Western chemical companies, after sharing pesticides, also brought in fertilizers, but without providing training in their proper use. Most people could not read the instructions even if they were written in local languages, and abusive chemical use combined with soil overuse to create new problems for farmers.

Left: *Smiling face of this Sherpani greets trekkers who come to her tearoom and lodge.*

Above: *Trinket shops such as these are found throughout the tourist towns of Nepal.*

Above: Subsistence farming provides livelihood as it has for generations.
Below right: Grain fields in Kingdom of Mustang in the northern region of Nepal.

Sustainability issues such as soil conservation and watershed management were named by the government as objectives 25 years ago but have not been pursued with continuity. Instead, wildlife reserves and national parks were established with the assistance of outside donors such as the World Bank/International Monetary Fund. The dependence on external aid has frequently derailed the government from its own proposed development plans. Deterioration of the soil and reduced crop yields resulted.

The world's eyes turned to saving the indigenous culture and communities of Nepal when musicians from Great Britain started singing of their plight. Artists for the Environment brought in funds from concerts and albums while educating the public. Others joined environmentalists and religious groups, such as climbers. One coalition undertook a community-based training and building project under a British forester, Chris Evans. In less than a decade, this small coalition established thirteen resource centers with a rich variety of fruits, vegetables, and fast-growing trees where hundreds of farmers were trained in sustainable agricultural methods. Few outsiders have given so much to the Nepalese as this conglomerate, except for one.

Above: *Terraces in valley of the Kingdom of Mustang.*

New Zealander Hillary first put Nepal on the map for hikers and climbers, and his zeal to preserve ancient traditions of the indigenous people and better their lives is legendary. His profound appreciation for the people grew from his dependence on them as a hiker. Close relationships with the Sherpa guides gave him a compassion for those who endured hardships and helped to maintain loyalty rarely encountered between people of different cultures and from different stations in life.

To many Western eyes, the Everest region is a place of great beauty and high mountains to be conquered. For the Sherpas who live there, however, life has few privileges. Hillary gave them what they needed. Hillary's Himalayan Trust has built 27 schools and 12 medical clinics, and has rebuilt the magnificent Tengbocke Monastery. The trust, partnered with the American Himalayan Foundation, has focused on supporting nunneries as well as monastic schools.

Right: *Porters working for trekkers on their way to Mount Everest.*

Above: *Fruit trees planted in reforestation effort of*
Annapurna Conservation Area Project.

Equally important is the tree planting undertaken by the trust, which supplies nearly 100,000 indigenous tree seedlings a year. Deforestation plagued the mountainous areas, as a result of both population pressures and tourism. Another outside group, the World Wildlife Fund, came to Nepal to save the endangered tigers but realized that the tigers' lives depended on the human community being saved. Along with local partners, the World Wildlife Fund is sponsoring and maintaining reforestation nurseries.

Community education became a primary activity for both the trust and the World Wildlife Fund through sponsorship of literacy classes and village tours. Conservation stories spread, and the groups learn from one another. New cooking and heating sources to conserve fuel have been introduced such as back-boilers, devices that use by-product heat energy from household cooking activities to heat water. Such basic appliances have done much to eliminate the need to cut trees.

Surprisingly, women have stepped forward with enthusiasm to learn the skills of tree nursery management and new methods to utilize the forests in a sustainable manner. Fruit trees and vegetables are becoming staples of Nepalese diets through their efforts, and associations called Mothers' Groups now educate girls in new farming techniques.

Below left: *Family farming in unchanged ways in Kangchenjunga region of Nepal.*
Above: *Family plowing, Everest region.*

That it was Hillary's Trust that first initiated the reforestation in Nepal and built alliances is not surprising. He cared, observed, and then took action. The humility and selflessness of this man cannot be overstated. He had once done the near impossible in climbing the world's tallest mountain and through his trust achieves the nearly impossible again, remaining loyal to an ideal and to a people he loved. Because of him, countless lives have been bettered and an entire culture is being preserved.

Mike Salomon follows in Hillary's footsteps. After a life-changing expedition near Everest in which a Sherpa guide saved him, Mike founded Sherpa Technology Guides, Inc. which donates five percent of its profits—and five percent of Mike's personal time—to helping a small village in Nepal that through his efforts now has a new bridge to connect it to a school, medical clinic, and market.

Recently, Sherpa Technology Guides, Inc., launched an initiative called the Adopt-a-Village Program to encourage other companies to help villages of the Himalayan region. The Nepalese government after decades of plans for large-scale improvements has developed a program that follows the model of the Western groups that have come to work with the people in their communities. The Annapurna Conservation Area Project (ACAP) focuses on participatory community-directed actions, promoting use of alternative energies to relieve deforestation for fuel wood. A profusion of water resources in the area offers great hydroelectric potential. When managed by local residents, the village-level micro-hydroelectricity plants are both economically viable and ecologically sound, and they teach sustainable practices in daily life.

The plights of both farmers and Sherpa guides have been improved through the intervention of caring outsiders and local government agencies, a partnership that has proven saving to this small and remote nation.

Above, top: *Deforestation in Lamjjura La, chopped wood in foreground.*
Below: *Chunkar poplars planted for fuel wood surround stuppa in the Mustang region.*
Opposite: *Tengboche monastery.*

CHAPTER FOUR

Save Our Coast and Rangeland Too

GAVIOTA, CALIFORNIA

> *"We simply need that wild country available to us, even if we never do more than drive to its edge and look in. For it can be a means of reassuring ourselves of our sanity as creatures, a part of the geography of hope."*
>
> *—Wallace Stegner from*
> Beyond the Hundredth Meridian

This magnificent blend of beautiful coastal bluffs and mountains is a mosaic of private, state, and federal land. I sat recently with a friend in its midst, breathing the scent of wind-blown saltwater and sage. We were two solitary souls, save for dolphins playing in the sea below and seagulls and pelicans flying above. The natural serenity of the scene implied that this 35-mile stretch of coastline was destined to remain open and free. Yet I knew that developers were again trying to take it over, piece by piece, attempting to urbanize the last remaining open coastline in southern California. Its proximity to Los Angeles and the population explosion in all parts of the state forecast a future of human encroachment. In protest, an alliance had been formed, composed of different people united by a common desire—to keep the area pristine.

Opposite: *The Gaviota coastline.*

I'd been introduced to the Gaviota Coast only recently, but my friend had always known its beaches. He had surfed there with his grade school chums. Those same children grew into adults, now fighting for every just cause that concerns them through a group they have formed called the Surfrider Foundation, propelled in their resolve by the fear of more jammed-together condominiums and more luxury homes, more golf courses. Other concerned citizens of many different factions in nearby Santa Barbara—including myself—have joined them.

Left: Sandpiper busy picking dinner out of sand at one of the many Gaviota beaches.
Below: Surfer waiting patiently as the sun sets.
Opposite: The inland areas of Gaviota Coast—sparse and unobstructed landscape, also the long-time grazing lands of resident ranchers.

Gaviota Coast ranchers at first protested against the efforts of the local Santa Barbara surfers and environmentalists who wanted to "save" the coast, declaring that there already were enough land-use regulations in place. The vast coastline and rolling hillsides are protected by numerous restrictions on further development; agriculture use is deemed the best use of the land in most areas. Despite this, housing development still threatens in the form of a project called "Naples," a "paper township" approved on a nineteenth-century surveyor's map.

Area farmers and ranchers know the land better than anyone else, sometimes through family ownership stemming back four generations. They know best how to be stewards of the land but have neither time nor opportunity to stay informed on issues of local development, and as a result, outsiders often subvert the laws in place. This is precisely what happened in the Naples Project, just as it had happened previously, down the coast a bit, when a new luxury hotel replaced a favorite beach spot formerly open to all.

Left and above: *Recreation, boating and biking, enjoyed by locals.*

Above: *Creek flowing through oakland after winter rains.*

The beginnings of ranching in California can be traced to its Mexican roots. Captain José de la Guerra acquired much of the land in the Gaviota area in 1837 in a land grant from Governor Juan Alvarado. A piece of this ranch later became the Rancho San Julian. The financial strain of ranching on less than ideal ranchland was primarily responsible for the breakup of large ranches. Over generations, tracts of Rancho San Julian were sold to pay mortgages and inheritance taxes. Today only a small portion of the original parcel remains, but it lives on in its entirety in photo archives going back many, many roundups. It is only through courage and loyalty to family history that a ranch such as the San Julian still exists and runs cattle.

When I visited the ranch I was immediately struck by its rich history. A. Dibblee Poet wrote a chronicle of his life there and of the excitement shared by the children of the San Julian as they participated in annual spring rodeos and cattle drives to the railroad.

This page: *Historic images of Rancho San Julian*
Opposite: *Historic painting of Rancho San Julian.*

RANCHO SAN JULIAN FROM THE SOUTH

Above: *Roundup of cattle down steep hillside in mid-twentieth century.*

Safeguarding California ranches safeguards the history of the state as well, as does the goal of preserving the pristine Gaviota Coast. Keith Zandona, a California surfer with his own construction business and president of the Surfrider Foundation, is dedicated to coastal preservation. Keith's crusade to save the Gaviota Coast goes back to 1968, when he first returned from military service in Vietnam, no longer cowed by authority. He remembers first attending a Santa Barbara County Board of Supervisors meeting to protest a new $1/a day fee for entrance to Jalama Beach, a place he had surfed since he was a little boy. Due in large part to his persistence, the board created the option of an annual fee, thus making the beach much more accessible for frequent and regular responsible use.

Keith went on to fight for Jalama Beach when Vandenberg Air Force Base attempted to move closer. His group, then called Save Our Coast, collected 17,000 signatures to present to the Board of Supervisors. He later met privately with some of the businesspeople interested in extending Vandenberg's stretch southward. They went on a field trip to discuss the proposal. While they walked along the beachfront, a red-tailed hawk flying overhead held a snake in its talons. "A good omen," Keith thought. And yes it was, for the business partnership at Vandenberg Air Force Base did not prevail.

When population and money press on farming interests, the ensuing conflict can lead to catastrophe for long-time inhabitants. For this reason the Surfrider Foundation, the Nature Conservancy, the local Audubon

Above: *Pounding surf off Gaviota Coast energizes surfers to fight for free access to beaches.*

Above: *Designation of a National Seashore would provide assurance of long-term permanent protections of these cliffs and beach on Gaviota Coast.*

Society, and the Chumash Indian tribe, among others, formed a broad-based alliance to enforce local nondevelopment ordinances that existed in the widespread community of ranches. During the past decade, the continual efforts of the Surfrider Foundation have prevented development despite the mega-resources of opponents. The group continues to present views at zoning hearings, planning meetings, Coastal Commission hearings, and wherever there is a need in cities from San Francisco to San Diego. Each battle has its own specific agenda, but there is only one underlying motivation: to defend the environment and the openness of the beaches.

The involvement of the surfers in an alliance that includes land trusts and conservancies as well as the Audubon Society and universities is not surprising when one considers that the people who make regular use of an area would naturally want it protected. Their closeness to the coast in their daily quest for the perfect wave has almost a spiritual element. The decades-old reputation of surfers as being either selfish kids or loners no longer applies.

Santa Barbara is a beautiful region, and the passion to keep it that way has provided the impetus for a continued struggle to keep developers out. Groups such as the Nature Conservancy and the Sierra Club have joined forces to create proactive long-term partnerships with various landowners and other stakeholders. Land conservancies have facilitated feasible alternatives to the sale of entire parcels. The preservation of the Arroyo Hondo Ranch, which could not continue as an agricultural enterprise, was one endeavor that answered many desires. It became a nature preserve—owned, operated, and funded by the Land Trust for Santa Barbara County. Schoolchildren go there now to picnic and play, and the endangered steelhead are again abundant in the streams.

Above: *Surfers played a major role in the alliance to protect the last remaining undeveloped coast in southern California. Their closeness to the coast in their daily quest for the perfect wave has almost a spiritual element.*

Above: *The rangeland of rolling hills and gently blowing grasses provided
the impetus for a continual struggle to keep developers out.*

Collaborative actions are becoming the standard. Even the Chumash tribe of Native Americans has become involved. Their ancestors had villages along the coast. For the Chumash, regaining the rights to those sites is not simply a legal matter but also a spiritual one. Eight thousand years ago a village of great archeological significance was inhabited along this coast. The Chumash today desire to build a school and a cultural center on sites in their ancestral homelands.

Guarding Gaviota requires a collaborative effort of all parties. Landowners, primarily ranchers, and groups concerned about long-term protection, primarily urban environmentalists, are engaging in the process of conversation and community building with respect to the mutual goal of protecting the Gaviota Coast.

Left: *Ranchers too joined the battle to protect their land and cattle from encroaching urbanization, though many preferred existing laws to the National Seashore designation.*
Left, below: *Typical ranch of Gaviota.*

Above: *Pleasant Valley, Yampa Valley Land Trust.*

CHAPTER FIVE

Cows, Not Condos

STEAMBOAT SPRINGS, COLORADO

> *"Those who contemplate the beauty of the earth find reserves of strength that will endure as long as life lasts."*
> *–Rachel Carlson, from*
> The Sense of Wonder

As the wind blew gently through my hair, butterflies and birds fluttered and flew, the children played, and I felt this little town was a very nice place. It was quiet, winter having ended and summer not yet begun. As I waited to meet Susan Dorsey Otis, director of the Yampa Valley Land Trust, I felt blessed. Here was a skiing town unlike any I had ever known, a town for the people who lived there, families and hot-shot skiers alike, and many ranchers.

For many years, Susan has dedicated her energies to the local ranchers. With the help of an East Coast land trust expert, she brought a vision to the area, a vision of a future in which the developers would not take over the open spaces of the ranches. The two women brought a method of implementing conservation: setting up land trusts.

Ranchers were the first to settle this Colorado region, followed by miners. Tourists eventually came, drawn to the healing spring waters, and skiers arrived in the last decades of the twentieth century. These newcomers did not change the basic ranching character of the region until the last decade or so when ranchers in increasing numbers sold off land.

At the same time that ranch land was being lost, changes in the town itself also concerned Susan and her friend Kathy. The trend of skiing towns had been set by other Rocky Mountain towns—towns grew exponentially from a single village to three or more towns. In Colorado, every hour of every day, four acres of wildlife habitat are gobbled up by development. In Steamboat, old-timers were not as interested in cash as newcomers who came to the area with their schemes to make an easy buck before moving on. The two women were determined to preserve local traditions and to conserve the land. Many residents attended town meetings to offer support to the two women's goal of conservation.

Susan is a warm and natural gal, but she is also the type to welcome a challenge. I was as struck by her ease and companionability as the ranchers must have been, ready to trust her competence. The Yampa Valley Land Trust was thus born from Susan Otis's many hours spent educating herself by volunteering at local planning and zoning meetings and then reaching out to ranchers to educate them. In time, the concept of giving portions of land to save it for future generations became an accepted concept. Land easements and whole parcels were donated to a trust managed by Yampa Valley ranchers themselves. Skiers too began to support the nongrowth or slow-growth approach for the area, even when it meant no future ski slopes would be developed.

Above: *The creation of another ski area like Steamboat Springs was not permitted. The locals decided that the plan so close down the valley would destroy the low-key, ranching atmosphere.*

Above: *Catamount Valley. The planned ski area was designed to become a major village of homes and a golf course beside the lake.*
Below: *Open space and cattle roaming, no cowboy pushing them away just now.*
Following spread: *The ranchland of Yampa Valley, preserved by the Yampa Valley Land Trust.*

Catamount Ski area, which had received preliminary approval, was the subject of intense discussion at town meetings as the date for final approval approached. Decisions were reached unlike any in other ski areas of the state. Determining the desired character of the town as well as the future economy of the area, longtime locals, seasonal ski residents, and ranchers realized they wanted things to stay the same, with open space and cattle roaming with the occasional cowboy among them.

Although by the end of the twentieth century the Wild West as portrayed in movies had vanished, Colorado towns remained places where laws and regulating agencies were not popular. Solutions to everyday matters came from the spirit of independence and self-reliance that are the primary characteristics of Steamboat Springs families; winters in the Rocky Mountains demanded toughness. Although the miners, ranchers, and skiers who came to Steamboat Springs were not as close-knit as in more established communities back East, they still talked, and the alliance born of the two women and area residents made decisions about the valley's future. The land was being split up as it was sold, and plans were being submitted that would permanently change their way of life. The common threat of development brought them together.

The townspeople of Steamboat Springs, though not distant in miles, were a different group. They had tolerated one another, recognizing some as local storeowners, some as old-timers, and some as transients for a season, but they were not the types to band together. In the early years the waters of hot springs lured tourists to the region. In 1974 a ski lift was introduced, and tourists no longer came for mere relaxation. For a week at a time all winter long, tourists check in, buy lift tickets, and head for the slopes. Those hired to serve them have mostly come for the winter season too, seeking skiing, drinking, dining, and making new friends.

Left, top and bottom: *Built-up town of Steamboat Springs.*

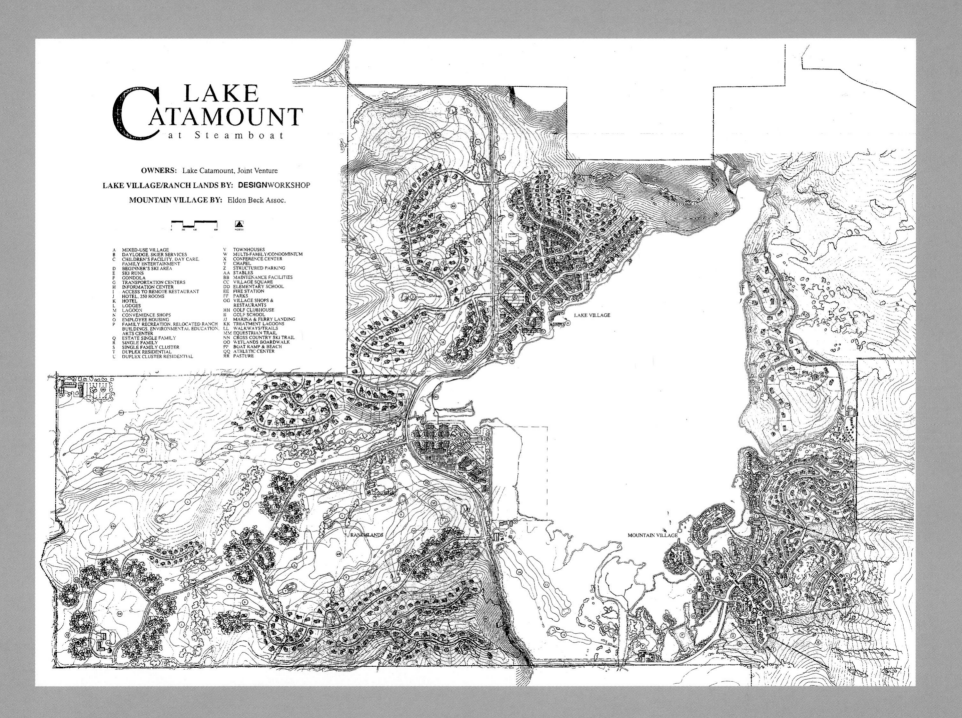

Above: *Catamount Valley preserved—no 3700 new homes or golf course or 1000-bed hotel as once planned.*

Above and opposite: *The Yampa River Valley preserved for cattle and cowboys. Just outside the commerce of Steamboat Springs ski area and town.*

Yet Steamboat Springs has been distinguished from other ski areas because of its ranching heritage. Although skiers rarely visit the ranches and ranchers don't often put on skis, a major winter event is the Annual Bud Light Cowboy Downhill Festival, featuring professional rodeo stars taking part in wacky ski races, drawing crowds from all parts of the state. The cowboy myth is a major part of Steamboat Springs' "ski marketing" as well as a summertime draw for families. Wild West Balloons, a local mom-and-pop operation, offers flights that give passengers "a taste of Steamboat Springs hospitality." The Western mystique is sold in every way, not only by dude ranches.

However, rugged mountainous terrain is not a place of entertainment for ranchers. Their livelihood depends on successful calving or getting through the haying before a rain. Yampa Valley ranchers are dedicated to work and have been hard-hit by falling beef prices. Avoiding the apparent ease of life in town, the rancher's work ethic is reinforced. To him, the freedom of wide-open spaces, the sweetness of the Yampa River, and the area's solitude are payment greater than cash. The pleasure of these things is in the blood, most of all after a hard day's work.

By the mid-1990s, the "glue" of history was not always enough to hold traditions in place. Ranching families were splitting, as elders died off and a younger generation chose a different life. Tax burdens increased, and easy cash from developers grew more attractive. The land itself was breaking up, marred by a series of cutaway zones for new roads and housing construction; the Western landscape was becoming a mess.

The U.S. Forest Service and the U.S. Army Corps of Engineers gave permits in the early 1970s to develop a new ski area, golf course, a lake and marina, 3,700 homes, and a 1,000-bed hotel. An entire new city had been proposed and approved eight miles south of Steamboat Springs. The costs to existing residents as a result of the increased population had not been considered. Although surveys had been taken in the community and opinion was strongly divided, years passed and plans moved closer to approval until the local Sierra Club threatened to sue. Because the town had no consensus and conservationists had no clout, ranchers led the protest campaign, in large part through the newly created Yampa Valley Land Trust.

Above: *Yampa River.*

This alliance also had to sell the idea of safeguarding the land to the people of Steamboat Springs, many of whom still wanted growth—more tourists, more ski runs, more business. It took a while for many to realize that tourists come to these mountains not for "more" but for what existed already. The "cowboy image" was one of open range land, meadows with flowers, working cowboys, and cattle. Tourists wanted to see and enjoy what was apparently fast disappearing. More golf courses and condos would turn them away. The value of the scenery was greater than the value of all the livestock and hay. It was also what the people discovered they needed for their own spirits and dreams; it didn't matter if they were locals, skiers, or ranchers.

Routt County, encompassing Steamboat Springs and the planned ski center Catamount, might become like other Rocky Mountain ski areas like Vail, commercialized and developed beyond recognition. In 25 years a valley of smog and traffic and towns had sprung from the original small village of Vail, and the people of Steamboat did not want to be next in line.

A committed group of residents, ranchers, skiers, and townsfolk spent thousands of hours over a span of years envisioning the community they wanted, learning along the way to express their own most deeply held values, eventually coming up with Vision 2020, an area community plan adopted with land trusts, conservation agreements, and a statement of shared vision.

The ranchers who first broke with the constraints of traditional ideas of ownership by donating their land to a land trust were some of the valley's oldest families. By giving certain rights to a separate entity, they saved estate taxes, assuring the future generation of the ability to maintain the ranches. Susan Otis phrased it: "Do you want to pay for additional growth, or do you want to pay for what is so special and unique about the community? It's not a difficult decision."

The landowners preserved their land by giving away 3,296 acres at Lake Catamount and putting in conservation easements to the Yampa Valley Land Trust in 1999. This decision was the death blow to the proposed ski resort community. Ranching operations continue today, and only a single lodge and 40 home sites in a conservation-oriented setting will be permitted in the natural grazing environment.

In May 2002, the local newspaper, "Steamboat Pilot," wrote that the area community plan adopted in 1995 has become the blueprint for all area development. The platform to go out and acquire open space, represented by the local bumper sticker "Cows, Not Condos," met the deep needs of a diverse populace. They had a vision for their land—to keep it the way it was.

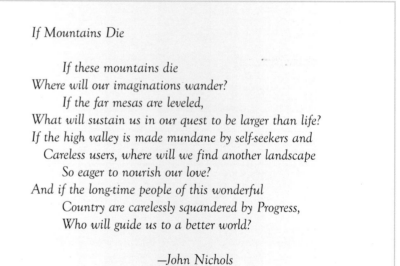

If Mountains Die

> *If these mountains die*
> *Where will our imaginations wander?*
> *If the far mesas are leveled,*
> *What will sustain us in our quest to be larger than life?*
> *If the high valley is made mundane by self-seekers and*
> *Careless users, where will we find another landscape*
> *So eager to nourish our love?*
> *And if the long-time people of this wonderful*
> *Country are carelessly squandered by Progress,*
> *Who will guide us to a better world?*

—John Nichols
If Mountains Die
(Taos, NM)

Above: Catamount.
Following spread: Yampa Valley Land Trust, with Catamount in the distance on the right.

Above: *Passenger ship, the M.S. Hanseatic, a cruise ship built to ice-strengthened standards, stopped from further exploration by sea ice in Antarctica.*

CHAPTER SIX

More Than Ice

ANTARCTICA

> "We came to probe the Antarctic's mystery, to reduce
> this land in terms of science, but there is always the
> indefinable which holds aloof yet rivets our souls."
> –Douglas Mawson, from
> Home of the Blizzard *(1915)*

A ntarctica is known as the Great White Continent, the Last Continent, and the Unknown Continent, Terra Incognita. For the tourist, it holds mystery and breathtaking beauty; for the scientist, it holds secrets. Antarctica is home to the last intact ecosystem to survive on the planet, and there is an unbelievable amount of activity of life beneath its frozen surface. There is also a myriad of mysteries locked away for eons in its ice chest.

Many superlatives are needed to describe a visit to Antarctica. For me, it was a most frightening and marvelous experience, for I had never known a more austere and more spiritual place. And it was clear that my fellow travelers, many in their 70s and even 80s, were similarly awe-inspired. From the very first evening of our nautical journey, we were drawn by the chill of the Arctic light, beckoned by its reflection in the ice. None of us had expected such intense amazement and wonder. The seasickness and bitter cold we endured during our three-week journey were a small price to pay for a glimpse of the mystical light beyond. We were adventurers, poets, like starry-eyed children eager with anticipation.

Above: White baby Weddell seal and mature elder.
The white color appears in approximately every 1000 seals.
Below right: *Chinstrap penguins, one of the many*
varieties of flightless bird that have wings that become
blades for swimming underwater.

Were the first voyagers to this southernmost ocean similarly entranced? I think not. The effort to survive must have been the only thought. Antarctica was the unknown continent in the nineteenth and early twentieth centuries, and most explorers came without items of comfort, without maps. Douglas Mawson, an Australian geologist who traveled in late 1912, was an expedition leader who wrote of the horrors of Antarctica. This, the windiest place in the world, took the lives of his dogs and both of his companions and left him barely alive. When rescuers found him he was so frostbitten and fatigued that he was unrecognizable. Mawson chronicled his memories of Antarctica in *Home of the Blizzard.* Other explorers of note include Scott Amundson, Robert Falcon Scott, and Ernest Shackleton, but it was eighteenth-century explorer James Cook of Great Britain who made "the far region" famous. Cook wrote of the abundance of marine life and the huge colonies of seals, starting the frenzied charge of hunters to the southern seas. The heroic explorations of these early travelers helped publicize the previously unknown waters and land of Antarctica.

For the next 100 years, Antarctica suffered the exploitation, pollution, and ecological disturbance of the human footprint. Hunters decimated both the seal and whale populations. In the late eighteenth century seals were the preferred catch, but as their population was depleted, whaling took over. Whales were used for food, for fuel, for women's corsets as boning. A growing technology gave rise to steam-powered ships and explosive harpoons, and the result was the large-scale slaughter of whales.

Above: *Gentoo penguins. Only the Gentoo penguins have expanded in any numbers in higher latitudes beyond the Antarctic Peninsula.*

Around the middle of the twentieth century, concerns over the shrinking whale population came to the fore. In 1946 the major whaling nations formed the International Whaling Commission (IWC). With the goal of protecting whales from becoming extinct, the Commission set quotas to restrict the number of whales killed. Despite this, the whale population continued to decline. Conservationists cried out for further restrictions. In 1982 the IWC voted to halt all killing of whales for a 10-year period. As the first agency to operate for the conservation of life in the Antarctic region, the IWC saved the whales from extinction. In doing so, it set the model for international cooperation in the protection of endangered species.

Many nations competed for a presence in Antarctica, but none tried to claim the land as its own. Despite world wars and continual bickering over land to the north, in the continent of Antarctica a different ethic prevailed—cooperation among nations and races. The international scientific community propelled the International Geophysical Year's focus on Antarctica in 1957. The International Council of Scientific Union and the Antarctic Treaty of 1961 followed.

Left: *Lemaire Channel steep rock walls, snow banks, and glaciers rise almost perpendicular to the narrow passage.*
Above: *King penguins.*

Above: *Pair of King penguins, protected by the Antarctic Treaty.*

Above: *Ice in sea before ice shelf and ice-covered mountain in Antarctica.*

Both of these agreements designated that Antarctica be used solely for scientific research and peaceful purposes. The Treaty of 1961 stated that "Antarctica shall be used for peaceful measures only in the interests of all humanity." The Protocol on Environmental Protection, signed in Madrid in 1991, imposed a 50-year moratorium on extracting oil and mining minerals. Signed by three times the number of signatories as the original, the Treaty of 1991 may be seen as testimony of the willingness of the world to abide in partnership.

There continue to be areas of contention. The French put in an air strip to serve their station, disregarding the breeding grounds of the penguin colony. The Japanese hunt the whales for "scientific" purposes, but whale meat appears at the dinner table of some high government officials. Continual monitoring by conservationists, some of whom have never been to Antarctica, aids the treaty when no other enforcement is effective. The cleanup of abandoned buildings and garbage at research stations and old whaling communities is a work in progress, but the millions of dollars that have been allocated promise to return the white land to its natural state.

Slowing climatic change to protect the icebergs of Antarctica is most essential for the fragile continent. The Kyoto Climate Treaty was signed by more than 170 countries, all agreeing to abide by detailed rules to reduce the greenhouse gases, but the Untied States walked away from the agreement. The World Wildlife Fund (WWF) has implemented a program called the Climate Savers to encourage corporations to pledge reductions in their carbon emissions. The nonprofit WWF has used scientific analysis, direct advocacy, public education, and the media to bolster support for the Kyoto Treaty. As the temperature of earth's atmosphere increases, so does that of the oceans, potentially to the melting point. In Antarctica, the recent breaking away of an iceberg the size of Massachusetts has alerted many more citizens to the dangers of procrastination.

Right: *Clouds enshrouding mountain peaks in Antarctica.*

In this most desolate land surrounding the South Pole the threat of encroachment by human predators will always exist. However, Antarctica's natural wilderness remains largely a pristine ecosystem of pre-human discovery. Curious penguins and playful seals, majestic icebergs and mystical ice in hues of deep blue and iridescent lavender—all appear to have inspired in humans a willingness to work together. In Antarctica, we humans may have rediscovered the concept of land as a gift and wildlife as an intrinsic part of that gift. The discoverer Captain Scott wrote these last words from his ice-bound tent in 1912: "For God's sake look after our people." I like to think he meant not only his family and friends at home but also the living world of Antarctica.

Top: Argentine station of Orcadas, the longest continually inhabited.
Above: Old whaling station of Grytviken, South Georgia, maintained as a historical site.
Right: Weddell seal pup.

Above: *Iceberg in the setting sun. Antarctica—the place. Scientists and universities might be competitors in the real world but here they are collaborators and colleagues, preserving and studying for the rest of the world.*

Aove: *Portland was a bustling city in the 1800s*

CHAPTER SEVEN

The City That People Love

PORTLAND, OREGON

> "I wish I had the time to tell you of the mighty possibilities of fair young Oregon. Her capacity for home is as unlimited as the azure of her skies on her fairest days. Her people are prosperous and progressive and their spirits are as free from fads as the air they breathe. They do not like professional agitators, but they love liberty."
>
> –Abigail Scott Dunway (1914)

"In the 1970s it was hard to foresee Portland's incipient dash for brilliance," in the words of Neil Peirce, nationally syndicated columnist, on the day he gave Portland leaders the Bruner Award for Urban Excellence in 1989. Portland's classic scenario as a dying city decades earlier had a different ending. Because citizens cared about their community, opposing groups were able to reach a consensus while government became an effective partner in achieving the city's renaissance. The city has been widely regarded as a model of urban renewal.

Portland's rebirth came about by gathering consensus to support broad alterations to the city's core, which had been losing its traditional commercial and residential markets to shopping malls and suburbs. The specific objective, stated by the Portland Design Committee, was "to create an urban community sufficiently attractive as a place to encourage citizens and activities in the immediate region to concentrate their energies and resources in the downtown." The goal was to make the downtown the best place to be.

Above and right: *Renewal of the transportation service was a key to the Redevelopment Plan of 1972.*
Opposite: *The "old" traffic system was largely congestion of private vehicles.*

Business leaders had been meeting as the "no name committee," worrying together about their loss of business to the suburbs. They officially became known as the Portland Improvement Committee the day each of those business executives chipped in $110,000 to pay for a professional study by an engineering/design firm.

Other elements of Portland had been meeting as well, protesting a plan by businessmen to erect a 12-story garage. Activists carrying "No Garage" signs to planning commission hearings had prevailed not many months before, and they emerged again in a chorus of countervoices responding to the plan of business interests. Garden clubs, environmentalist groups, artists, and architects had different ideas.

Portland has a history of neighborhood groups acting independently from city hall. The 1960s were an era nationwide of rising citizen participation, and a small revolution of citizens in Portland, epitomized by Riverfront for People, had begun working in the neighborhoods in grassroots advocacy groups. This alliance of residents and downtown business leaders in 1972 made the transformation of Portland envisioned in the renewal plan a viable, successful reality. In less than two years, the city had agreed on a Redevelopment Plan that has served a model for other cities around the country.

Top: *The Willamette River, largely inaccessible to the public.*
Above: *Waterfront Park opened the river to the people.*

The Portland plan focused on community involvement with neighborhood councils, architects, and planners. Three individuals are prime examples of the three-part planning process that succeeded: William Roberts, a second-generation department store owner and holder of landmark office buildings, who loved the quiet of back-room conversations almost as much as he liked to hunt and fish is the woodsy areas of his state; Rodney O'Hiser, an architect made lead organizer, who held unofficial diplomatic skills for handling the awkward, almost argumentative situations that continued to arise; and Isabell Ashcroft, a retired teacher who resided in one of the changing neighborhoods and who, despite her years, was an active, vigilant participant to whom city builders listened.

The transformation began with a celebration called Dreamspan, which centered on the Willamette River as a visual symbol of unity. The major bridge crossing was closed for a day to allow people to walk, bike, or tour by boat and bus in order to see the city in as many ways as possible and to get excited about the new planning effort. Afterwards, workshops that included children were held throughout the city. When completed, Dreamspan involved over 10,000 people from grandparents to grandchildren, from professionals to laypeople. What emerged was a vision of the city without a freeway near the river and without the barrier between downtown and the river's banks. Residents clearly wanted a city that provided access to the richness of theaters and museums, restaurants and shopping.

Neighborhoods were represented in a broadly based committee, the Citizen's Advisory Committee (CAC), which the mayor conceived. Over the course of fourteen months, the CAC acted as a third party, separate from city hall and business, dealing with the proliferation of groups that sprang up in response to the planning process. Citizens for a Car-Free Inner City, Save the Fourcourt Fountain, and a group promoting electric transit were just a few of these groups. STOP (Sensible Transport Options for People) emerged as a powerful voice in determining the city's future.

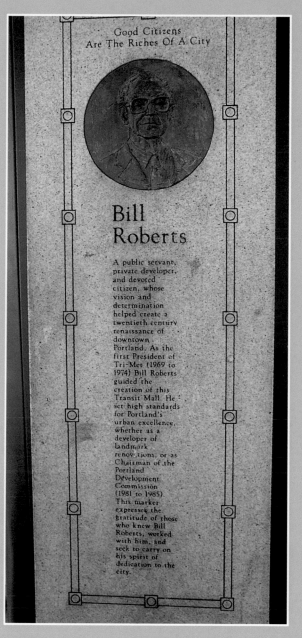

Above: *Plaque placed as a memorial on the Bill Roberts Transit Mall. Bill was born and raised in Portland and was appointed the first chairman of the Tri-Met Board for Transportation, following a long career in department stores. He was driven by a vision that included art, historic lamps, and attractive bus shelters and was widely respected for his integrity and fairness. He played a major role in guiding Portland's downtown renewal. The plaque reads "Good Citizens Are The Riches Of A City."*

Above: *A fountain of water for all in Waterfront Park.*

Wide public participation in policy development was the key element to the successful renewal of Portland's downtown. Another key element, almost as important, was the momentum of the planning process. The essential ideas of the plan were developed over a fourteen-month period, an intense time of active public involvement and much media attention. The city "declared its intentions" and then began to implement the essential public features of the plan: closing a freeway to create a waterfront park; building the transit mall; creating a public square to replace an old parking area in the retail core. The mayor's aggressive style was perfect for the needs of the time.

In the wake of controversy and disappointment in the 1960s over public involvement in the war on poverty, citizen electoral participation in Portland took on new energy by electing a new mayor and city council, all young individuals. An increase in middle-class, educated organizers also set the stage for the renewal project of the 1970s. CAC fostered a dynamic grassroots process as task forces formed to develop goals and objectives for the plan. Regular newsletters kept people abreast of every detail, and final documents were adopted by consensus. The CAC was required to review all development proposals for the Planning Committee to ensure that the plan's support was not lost along the way.

Public funds were wisely spent, encouraging private development. Portland succeeded because it had a process driven by a shared vision of a revitalized city. One of the city commissioners at the time, Margaret Strachan, stated in a speech: "The process we're using is turning the traditional planning role upside down. It starts with the citizens, is driven by them, is controlled by them, and is approved by them. The planner serves as a guide, skilled professional, and pencil for the public."

The riverfront was given a park, and the public was given mass transit to replace the old bus system. A transit mall with broad sidewalks, trees and sculptures provided a pleasant, rich, and diverse pedestrian experience. Another achieved goal was "to provide for the humanization of the downtown through promotion of the arts and excellence of design." The Waterfront Park and the Pioneer Courthouse Square and Transit Mall with light rail were the outcome of many more years of planning and negotiating.

Waterfront Park at first met with disapproval from the State Highway Department, which fought the removal of the existing Harbor Drive. But the 1972 plan at last won the department over, and the road was replaced by green space and the riverfront was opened to the people.

Above: *The old hotel that was replaced by a garage that was replaced by Pioneer Square in downtown Portland.*

Above and right: *Oregon's wildlife and art in downtown Portland.*

Initially, the piazza concept for Pioneer Courthouse Square met with disapproval at the higher levels because businessmen feared that the open brick courtyard would invite too many "undesirable" types and not provide enough security. Such an intensely open public space was contrary to conventional planning patterns in the United States but was common in Europe. Although the newly elected mayor declared the idea "dead," a citizens' fund-raising committee, the Friends of Pioneer Square, came up with an innovative promotional idea—selling personalized bricks for the planned plaza. The group also marketed the plaza by "selling" such architectural features of the square as columns, drinking fountains, trees, and trash receptacles. In the end the group raised $1.2 million, and public funds followed when a nonprofit organization was appointed to manage and operate the square. The inauguration of the new center of the city of Portland was held April 6, 1984.

Portland's example to other cities lies in the unity of citizens and government, planning with the planners, being the planners. Businessmen and citizens worked out differences in small committees and brought resolutions to higher committees, finally offering a viable outcome for architects and planners.

The creation of "unlikely partnerships" was the key to Portland's success, with citizens, officials, and business leaders sharing the dream of a renewed city throughout the long process.

On a practical level, the democratic principles on which the United States is based were given a living form. In Portland, as Abigail Dunway observed, "they love liberty."

Above: *Pioneer Square, the downtown center for people to enjoy.*

CHAPTER EIGHT

A Blueprint for Ecological Design

CURITIBA, BRAZIL

> *"Good examples and policies will build up and capture the imagination. At some point the imagination of whole cities will kick into gear."*
>
> –Richard Register, from
> Ecocities: Building Cities
> in Balance with Nature

Thirty years ago, Curitiba was like many South American cities–crowded, struggling with unemployment, and with little hope for change. Today, while still not a prosperous city, the residents claim they like it very much. What happened?

Jaime Lerner, a former architectural student trained in urban planning, was elected mayor of Curitiba. With all the resilience and impetuousness of youth, Lerner embarked on the ambitious creation of an eco-city. It all began one weekend after Lerner proposed a pedestrian mall to replace a central street. The public, shopkeepers, and public administration employees all objected, not ever having seen a pedestrian mall.

Opposite: *Rua das Flores, or Avenue of Flowers. Mayor Lerner's proposal to turn a major central street into a pedestrian mall was initially met by an outcry of opposition. Now the pedestrian mall is filled with busy shops and shoppers.*

Rather than wait for approval, Lerner and his architect friends decided to start one Friday night and be finished by Monday morning. They pulled up the street, put down cobblestones and kiosks, and provided thousands of pots of flowers. More important, they put down clean white paper and brought in children, gave them crayons, and told them to begin coloring. No police could drive though what appeared to be a playground, and by the next day, when shopkeepers had even more customers than before, opposition ended.

This action started a political pattern. Lerner worked with the children as his partners in nonviolent protests and as teachers. City projects were first geared to appeal to the youngsters, who were less invested in the established ways and eager to do what was new. Elders were taken by surprise by the new mayor's imaginative approach, but children caught on immediately and were delighted.

Right: *The crowded central street is now the pedestrian mall of Rua das Floras, above.*

Above: *Parade fills Rua das Floras.*

Lerner intended to make the city a place that enticed people into its center. He spoke first of environment and education, focusing on transformation of the transportation system to foster both. Lerner and his friends were planners as well as architects, and thinking of the city's future, they immediately encountered the problem of crowded streets. Although dismantling the buildings and streets that existed to build highways through the city had been the plan of the previous administrators, the new team thought differently. Old buildings, they thought, should be preserved and new roads built to encourage riding buses.

Five structural arteries with special lanes set up for speed diverted traffic away from the city center. Bus lines were established with new tripartite buses, color-coded for ease of recognition. New Plexiglas tubular stations were introduced that eased the loading of commuters onto buses. After several years, Curitiba had a transportation system that equaled New York City's subways—with a much smaller budget.

By ridding the downtown of traffic, pedestrian malls became a pleasant shopping experience. One street, Rua das Flores, became filled with shoppers and pots of flowers tended by children. Curitiba's inclusion of young people is helping to create future responsible citizens.

The reduction of more than 25 percent of downtown traffic spared residents pollution as well. The ingenious planning of major thoroughfares that extend from the city center was matched by thoughtful zoning of commercial and residential use. Old buildings were saved, designated for renovation and new uses. Lerner promoted city growth along the trail of memory and of transport, believing that "memory is the identity of the city and transport is the future."

Opposite: *Curitiba's new transportation system features major arteries or thoroughfares leading downtown.*
Top and above: *Tripartite buses are like subways, transporting large numbers at high speeds. Plexiglass tubular stations ease commuter loading onto buses.*

Another highlight of Curitiba's new eco-city is the abundance of green space, the result of a parks program that has created 550 feet of open space for every citizen. Given a limited budget, planners again thought cheap and simple, supplying 1.5 million tree seedlings to neighborhood residents to plant and maintain. By involving citizens as planters, the project promoted ecological awareness and neighborhood pride.

Above, top: *Park walkway.*
Above: *Lakes in parks are part of flood control.*
Opposite: *Curitiba used flood-planning federal funding to also build recreation facilities. The inner city tennis courts and parks are part of these revenues.*

A similar approach to schooling is remarkable for its simplicity and effectiveness. Old schoolbuses were recycled into classrooms and made available to adults as well as children, then settled on the edges of neighborhoods. Short-term courses to teach technical skills for employment were begun, and the Open University was opened in the town center.

Although education isn't free, it is quite inexpensive. Those who were unemployed at first, including the migrants from the rural areas, learned that they could pick up garbage for recycling in exchange for food and a small salary to attend school. Rural peasants were given opportunity and quickly became integrated into the city's life.

Another urban community model that gained international attention is that of the "green exchange" recycling program in which residents dress up as trees to go into schools and teach children about the power of recycling. The saving of trees and benefits of the green exchange were made very real to the children with a minimum of advertising. The children's support was further gained by giving out pictures of their heroes in exchange for non-biodegradable trash. They could identify themselves as "heroes for saving the planet." Guided by the "garbage that's not garbage" slogan, Curitiba residents currently recycle 70 percent of the city's trash.

It is tempting to see the story of Curitiba as the revolutionary activity of a single man and his friends. Such is not the case, although the strength of perception and ability to act quickly and simply that Lerner applied as mayor cannot be underestimated. He responded to the city's series of public debates in 1965 called Curitiba de Amanha (Curitiba of Tomorrow), and partnership between citizens and government became a reality.

Lerner worked with a citizenry that shared a history of active political involvement despite poverty and low literacy levels. Residents were grateful and proud to support a new Opera House and ideas for green space. When Lerner was elected in 1971, he was not expected to do anything special; this was, after all, the pattern of mayors before him in this military-ruled country. But he surprised everyone. He was a man who saw opportunities or made them. A typical example was Lerner's view of the country's recent passage of a flood abatement incentive act as an opportunity to build parks. Water could be diverted into new lakes in parks, solving flooding and at the same time protecting natural habitats of valley floors and riverbanks. Parks eventually provided recreation areas such as tennis courts and rivers, right next to office buildings. While other Brazilian cities undertook large, expensive flood-control projects they couldn't complete, Curitiba received federal money for realistic, smaller-scale projects that served both recreational and practical purposes.

Left: Part of Curitiba's education plan, the Open University, rising from an old quarry pit.

Recreational open space within the newly developing commercial and residential areas was facilitated not only by federal monies but also by neighborhood support. Curitiba got residents and businesses involved through inexpensive initiatives that matched their needs with planning objectives. For instance, Curitiba recycled nineteenth-century industrial buildings into cultural centers such as the city's showcase Opera Hemerges, built in an abandoned quarry. A waterfall, previously a part of the mining operation, flanks the modern steel and glass construction in the center of town. No attempt was made to cover the old quarry. The Open University was similarly placed in the middle of the city, rising out of an old quarry pit, created by the city to serve the residents with education of all types; short courses are available to build employment skills, longer classes address historical and cultural interests.

Lerner also became known for the speed with which he accomplished tremendous projects, such as building the Opera House in a month or closing a major street and creating a pedestrian mall over a weekend. Where administrative delays bog down most city planners, Lerner took steps first and dealt with complications later.

Curitiba's current challenge lies in maintaining sustainable development for a growing population. To further this goal, neighborhood centers seek input from residents and share the information with higher government agencies. Schools promote a well-educated citizenry, and businesses now cooperate and form associations. Protecting the environment has become a positive daily commitment for young and old, professional and citizen.

Just as in Portland, Oregon, land-use planning and urban transportation improvement in this Brazilian eco-city have been treated as two sides of the same coin necessary to the city's plan for change.

Planners were "visionaries" and architects became "tree people." The energy of workers who knew no ordinary boundaries left behind a city of pedestrian malls instead of streets, parks instead of shantytowns, and an Opera House and an Open University where a quarry used to be. A blueprint for an eco-city was born of a mayor who partnered with children, planners, and migrant workers. Without these partnerships, the innovative solutions would not have been found.

With a population of over three million, Curitiba has nearly doubled in size since Lerner first came to office, and yet the community continues to be innovative in planning and developing its parks and transportation system. Six more parks, a botanical garden, and eight wooded areas have been added, totaling more than eight million square meters of public nature space that is preserved for future generations.

Opposite and above: *Botanical garden in Curitiba's central city, part of parks program of eight million meters of public nature space preserved for future generations.*

Sources and Credits

Chapter 1
For the Birds

Delta Waterfowl Foundation
P.O. Box 3128
Bismarck, ND 58502
(888) 987-3695
(877) 667-5656 (Canada)
www.deltawaterfowl.org

Ducks Unlimited Canada
P.O. Box 1150
Stonewall, MB Canada
R0C 2Z0
(800) 605-Duck (3825)
www.ducks.ca

North Dakota Fish & Game
100 W. Bismarck Expressway
Bismarck, ND 58501-5095
(701) 328-6300
www.state.nd.us/gnf/

Ducks Unlimited, Inc.
One Waterfowl Way
Memphis, TN 38120
(800) 45Ducks
www.ducksunlt.org

National Assoc. of Conservation
Districts
509 Capitol Court, NE
Washington, DC 20002-4946
(202) 547-6450
www.nacdnet.org

So. Dakota Farm Bureau
Federation
P.O. Box 1426
Huron, SD 57350
(605) 353-8050
http://fb.org

Chapter 2
Iceland

California Fuel Cell Partnership
3300 Industrial Blvd., Ste. 1000
West Sacramento, CA 95691
(916) 371-2870
www.fuelcellpartnership.org

Iceland Review Daily News
Heimur hf.
Borgartuni 23
105 Reykjavik, Iceland

Sierra Club
85 Second Street, Second Floor
San Francisco, CA 94105-3441
(415) 977-5500
http://www.sierraclub.org/pow-
erlunch/

Icelandic New Energy Ltd.
Sidumula 13
P.O. Box 8192
128 Reykjavik, Iceland
(+354) 588-0310
www.newenergy.is

Shell Hydrogen
P.O. Box 38000
1030 BN
Amsterdam, The Netherlands
(+31) 20 630 9111
www.shell.com/hydrogen/

World Business Council for
Sustainable Development
4 chemin de Conches
1231 Conches-Geneva,
Switzerland
(+41) (22) 839 31 00
http://www.wbcsd.com/

Chapter 3
Nepal

American Himalayan
Foundation
909 Montgomery St., Suite 400
San Francisco, CA 94133
(415) 288-7245
www.himalayan-foundation.org

Himalayan Trust
Lowecroft, Plains Lane
Blackbrook, Belper, Derby's
DE56 2DD
England
www.eshopone.co.uk

World Wildlife Fund
1250 Twenty-Fourth Street, NW
Washington, DC 20037
(800) 960-0993
http://www.wwfnepal.org

Himalayan Explorers
Connection
P.O. Box 3665
Boulder, CO 20307
(303) 998-1007
http://hec.org

MS Nepal
Dillibazar
GPO 4010
Kathmandu, Nepal
(977) 1-434040
www.msnepal.org

Mountain Institute, Inc.
1828 L St., NW
Washington, DC 20036
http://www.mountain.org

Chapter 4
Gaviota

Audubon Society
Goleta Chapter
5679 Hollister Ave., Suite 5B
Goleta, CA 93117
(805) 507-1115

Land Trust of Santa Barbara
P.O. Box 91830
Santa Barbara, CA 93190-1830
(805) 966-4520

Surfrider Foundation
122 S. El Camino Real, PMB#67
San Clemente, CA 92672-4043
(800) 743-surf
www.surfrider.org

Gaviota Coast Conservancy
P.O. Box 1099
Goleta, CA 93116
http://www.gaviotacoast.org
www.gaviotacoast.org

Santa Barbara Farm Bureau
P.O. Box 1846
Buellton, CA 93427
(805) 688-7479
www.cfbf.com

Chapter 5
Steamboat Springs

American Farmland Trust
1200 18th St., NW, Suite 800
Washington, DC 20036
(202) 331-7300
www.farmland.org

Colorado Open
274 Union Blvd., Suite 320
Lakewood, CO 80228
(303) 988-2373
http://coloradoopenlands.org

Nature Conservancy of Colorado
P.O. Box 775528
Steamboat Springs,
CO 80477-5528
www.tnccolorado.org

Colorado Division of Wildlife
Habitat Partnership Program
Colorado Dept. of Natural
Resources
(303) 866-2607
http://dnr.state-co.us

High Country News
P.O. Box 1090
Paonia, CO 81428
(970) 527-4898
www.hcn.org

Yampa Valley Land Trust
P.O. Box 773014
Steamboat Springs, CO 80477
(970) 879-7240
www.yvlt.org

Chapter 6
Antarctica

British Antarctic Survey
High Cross, Madingley Road
Cambridge
CB3 0ET
United Kingdom
44 (0) 1223 221400
http://www.antarctica.ac.uk

National Science Foundation
4201 Wilson Blvd.
Arlington, VA 22230
(703) 292-5111
http://www.nsf.gov/

Tiger
USRA/NASA/GSFC Code 661
Greenbelt, MD 20720
(301) 286-1041
http://tiger.gsfc.nasa.gov/questions.html

Falklands Conservation
1 Princess Avenue
Finchley, London N3 2DA
United Kingdom
http://falklandsconservation.com/AboutFC/membership.html

Passport to Knowledge
P.O. Box 1502
Summit, NJ 07902-1502
http://passport.arc.nasa.gov/antarctica2/main/order.html

Chapter 7
Portland

Ecotrust
721 NW Ninth Avenue, Ste. 200
Portland, OR 97209
(503) 227-6225
http://www.ecotrust.org/connect

Oregon Historical Society
1200 SW Park Avenue
Portland, OR 97205-2483
orhist@ohs.org

Portland Parks & Recreation
1120 SW Fifth Ave., Ste. 1302
Portland, OR 97204
(503) 823-PLAY
http://www.portlandparks.org/waterfrontpark/issues
challenge.htm

1000 Friends of Oregon
534 SW Third Avenue, Ste. 300
Portland, OR 97204
(503) 497-1000
info@friends.org

Portland Development
Commission
1900 SW Fourth Ave., Ste. 7000
Portland, OR 97201-5304
http://www.pdc.us/url

Chapter 8
Curitiba

Bus Rapid Transit
http://www.fta.dot.gov/brt/issues/pt5.html

Eco-City Builders
1678 Shattuck Avenue
Berkeley, CA 94709
.Ecocity@igc.org

The International Network of
Green Planners
P.O. Box 221
NL 4140 AE Leerdam
The Netherlands
31-345-641927
http://www.ingp.org

Curitiba Municipal Perfect
http://www.curitiba.pr.gov

Institute of Development Studies
University of Sussex
Brighton BN 1 9RE, UK
44(0) 1273 606261
ids@ids.ac.uk

Credits

Book Design:
Peggy Ferris Design
Santa Barbara, CA

Editing:
Susan Gardner
Abby George

Photography Credits

All photos are by Tim Hauf
except:

Page	Photographer
2-3:	Bill Cain
6-9:	©Rich Reid, Colorsofnature.com
16:	Fred Greenslade
18:	Fred Greenslade (Mallard)
20:	Karen Roberts
21:	Fred Greenslade
48-53:	Rich Reid
54-56:	Rancho San Julian archives
57-59:	Rich Reid
60-61:	Dibblee Hoyt
64:	postcard
76:	Orion Knox
78:	Karen Roberts
79:	Oriion Knox
80-81:	Bill Cain
81:	Karen Roberts (penguins)
82:	Orion Knox
83:	Karen Roberts
84-85:	Bill Cain
86:	Karen Roberts
87:	Bill Cain
88, 91:	Oregon Historic Society
92:	inset—Oregon Historic Society
95:	Oregon Historical Society
90:	Curitiba Library
100:	Curitiba Library (small b/w)
105:	inset—Curitiba Library